I0470734

Preparing for the Fiscal Cliff

Vincent Bernhardt

Marcella Bernhardt

Copyright © 2012 Vincent Bernhardt, Marcella Bernhardt

All rights reserved.

ISBN: 1490372466
ISBN-13: 978-1490372464

DEDICATION

To all our family and friends. Thank you for believing in us..

TABLE OF CONTENTS

INTRODUCTION

In late summer of 2012 we went to a conference (it wasn't even a financial conference) and one of the speakers ominously mentioned "the fiscal cliff." We looked at each other and asked "What can we do to prepare for this?"

For the next few weeks we asked our friends, many of them much more financially literate than we are, and none of them had any advice. Some heard of the fiscal cliff and some could even tell us what comprised part of the cliff, but they didn't have any good advice on what to do.

We asked family members and received the same response. So we had to look at each other and wonder - if our family and friends have no idea how to prepare for the fiscal cliff, what chance do any of us have to actually survive it?

Quite often the common method of dealing with what life gives you is to simply ignore what is happening and hope for the best. Hope is not a plan.

We're pretty good at research and decided we should find out what we could do to prepare. What we found surprised, shocked and dismayed us.

We decided we needed to put all the information we gathered into something coherent and it became this book. The original idea was to put it together and get a copy to our brothers and their families, to our children and to all our friends.

The problem is that we are starting pretty late in the game. Now we are into Fall of 2012 and we launch off the cliff on New Year's Day, 2013. As you'll see, however, it isn't hopeless, even though it is pretty grim.

There are many things you can do before the end of 2012 to prepare for this financial crisis that will catapult most American families into economically tougher times. This book will help you figure out what some of those things are.

Other tasks are longer term, but worthwhile. Some scenarios are stark, but most mitigate the fiscal cliff somewhat. After all, the American people have suffered financially for a long time and facing tough times is still what we do, as a country and as individuals.

Not all this advice will work for everyone. This book is intended to provide a guideline, with specific things you can do that will help in 2013 and beyond. Some of the advice, such as get out of debt, is good, solid advice for everyone at any time, but especially relevant now.

We hope this book helps you.

THE FISCAL CLIFF LOOMS

Federal Reserve Chairman Ben Bernanke coined the term "fiscal cliff" to describe the potential financial crisis pending in the United States at the be beginning of 2013. Others have given this crisis a different name: Taxmageddon. According to the Congressional Budget Office (CBO) the latest budget outlook reduces the federal deficit by approximately half a trillion dollars during the 2013 fiscal year. The drop from 2012 federal deficits to the baseline deficits in 2013 is what makes this financial cliff so dramatic, most likely sending America back into a recession. There are many underlying causes for this financial crisis and they all affect you.

Effective on New Year's Day, January 1, 2013, a large number of significant financial provisions for the typical American will expire. For example, every American taking home a paycheck will immediately take home two percent less. We'll cover the reasons shortly, but this isn't the only component of the fiscal cliff. Other financial disasters loom for the average American. If Congress does not act, the immediate effects can be devastating.

The currently funded national debt is about $16 trillion. This does not include the unfunded liabilities of the Treasury, which are significantly larger than that. The scary part is that these unfunded liabilities include Social Security and Medicare, affecting millions of Americans. So far the only reason the United States can manage this huge debt is because of the low interest rate, which is less than two percent. Still, even at this low percentage, the debt service level is $300 billion per year, an amount most government officials feel is reasonable.

Americans are caught between a rock and a hard place at the edge of this cliff (are we mixing metaphors?). On the one hand, the government is curtailing spending by about $1.2 trillion dollars (by itself, not a bad thing to do). On the other hand, the Bush-era tax cuts expire at the same time, increasing the effective taxes on capital gains and dividends. These two components will remove about $600 billion dollars from the domestic economy.

If Congress doesn't act, and act decisively, Americans will face a financial crisis that threatens to cause an economic and social implosion across this great nation. Yet even if Congress moves to mitigate some of the upcoming causes of this fiscal cliff, the American taxpayer still faces significant financial trials in the future. You need to plan for higher taxes and expect market volatility.

What can you do to prepare for this fiscal cliff? There isn't much time left, yet there are many things each of us can do to protect ourselves, our families and our incomes. These are not all easy decisions, and not all suggestions are applicable to everyone, but preparing in some manner for the long-term financial changes that will affect you is still a wise thing to do.

"The looming fiscal cliff threatens to boost taxes by more than $500 billion in 2013 when many temporary tax provisions are scheduled to expire. Nearly 90 percent of Americans would pay more tax, primarily because the temporary cut in Social Security taxes and many of the 2001/2003 tax cuts would expire. Low-income households would pay more due to expiration of tax credits in the 2009 stimulus. High-income households would be hit hard by higher tax rates on ordinary income, capital gains, and dividends and by the new health reform taxes. And marginal tax rates would rise, potentially affecting economic decisions."[i]

Most American families, making between $40,000 and $60,000 per year will get hit by an extra $2000 in taxes in 2013, possibly a bit more. What many economists fear is that going over the fiscal cliff will extend the current recession, perhaps even deepening it. Not only will more people lose jobs (due in large part to belt-tightening in many businesses) but worker morale will be further eroded. This can lead to loss of a competitive edge in the United States and investment capital fleeing the country.

"As the cliff approaches, we expect first firms and then households to start positioning decisions, weakening the economy in advance of the cliff. When you are approaching a cliff, in a deep fog of uncertainty, you slow down," Bank of America Corp. (NYSE: BAC) economists wrote in an early June, 2012 report.

COMPONENTS OF THE CLIFF

There are many factors involved in the potential fiscal dilemma. Unfortunately, almost all of them adversely affect the finances of the American family. In order to plan how to protect yourself and your money, you need to know what these factors are.

We mentioned earlier that Americans taking home a paycheck will see an immediate two percent drop in their take-home pay. Last February Congress extended a two-percent decrease in the Social Security payroll deduction. The amount deducted from your paycheck to pay for Social Security was 4.2%. Unless Congress extends the cut again, and they probably won't, that amount will become 6.2%. This will affect about 160 million Americans.

The Earned Income Tax Credit is automatically scaled back in 2013. Currently couples making $19,190 or less receive $475 per year, and this benefit increases for each child. Lower income households will be hit hard by this.

For married couples, the "marriage penalty reduction," part of the Bush tax cuts, also expires. This enabled average American couples to pay less taxes filing jointly than separately. When this expires couples will once again face an increase in taxes if they choose to file jointly.

For those unfortunate struggling Americans using unemployment benefits, the news is even worse. The federal extension of unemployment benefits is another program expected to expire. Those who get laid off in 2013 will no longer be able to receive a maximum of 99 weeks of benefits, allowed by the existing plan, but will be limited to the original maximum of 26 weeks of unemployment benefits.

The dependent children tax deductions will be cut in half, from $1000 to only $500. Obviously families with many children will be hit hard by this.

The American Opportunity Tax Credit, giving families with college-enrolled dependents a small deduction for all four years of college, also expires. The Hope Credit remains, but it is for a smaller deduction and for only two years of college.

Some programs with dedicated funds are targeted for a reduction in funding. Medicare faces a two percent drop in their budget, which will ripple through the health industry, especially as our population ages.

Every "discretionary" program, those without earmarked funds, faces an 8% budget cut. This means federally-funded programs will scale back on spending, not necessarily a bad thing. However, we take many of these programs for granted, among them schools, roads and public health.

The Bush tax cuts expire, meaning higher taxes on capital gains and dividend income. Though this may seem to affect only higher-income Americans, most citizens have pension and profit sharing plans that are directly affected by these taxes.

The Alternative Minimum Tax expires, which it does every year, but if Congress does not extend this AMT, many middle-class Americans will be hit with a tax designed for the wealthy.

Estate and gift taxes will increase. Estate taxes will revert from a $5 million exemption with a 35% rate to a $1 million exemption with a 55% rate.

Automatic cuts in defense spending will occur. In this sequester, defense contractors are hit hardest, but most federal defense agencies still face about an 8% cut in budget. Many private, civic and nonprofit programs funded by the government will also face reductions, though they will probably be smaller. Many Americans depending on government checks, directly or indirectly, will be affected.

The Affordable Care Act (Obamacare) is funded in large measure by a capital gains tax of 3.8%. That is not, however, where all the funding comes from. A new tax to pay for the health care plan will directly impact unearned income for Americans making more than $250,000 per year. New taxes on sales of property will also take effect.

This is by no means a complete and total listing of all the impacts, but should represent the major ones of import to the average American.

These combined tax increases and spending cuts reflect a $600 billion reduction in the Gross Domestic Product of the United States, or about 3.5% of the anticipated $16 trillion for 2013.

Wikipedia[ii] defines "Gross Domestic Product (GDP) is the market value of all officially recognized final goods and services produced within a country in a given period." You have less money to spend on yourself and your family. You become fearful. Spending decreases in society which puts less money into circulation. In Systems, that's a downward spiral, or Escalation Archetype. In normal conversation, that's a recession.

WHAT TO EXPECT

There is much information on what the fiscal cliff is, though that information is scattered across hundreds of websites. There is a little less information on what we can actually expect in the beginning of 2013. One thing seems clear; if Congress does not act the American public will get pounded economically. As many people point out, if Congress does nothing, the United States debt and deficit problems will greatly impact the economy. That is not a good prospect for any of us.

Congress almost always waits until the last possible moment to make difficult choices. In this case, pressures to safeguard the economic well-being of the United States will force Congress to make budget compromises.

Congress will probably step in and make some changes, pushing the timing of the fiscal cliff further out. Make no mistake, though, this defers the problem and does not eliminate it. Still, instead of a single financial drop in the economy of the United States, we can expect a number of smaller drops. The financial numbers push us down a hill in that case, instead of dropping us off a cliff.

The Congressional Budget Office[iii] is a non-partisan entity that tries to diligently assess the condition of the United States economy. In one report they state "If the government continues to print money, the policy would lead to hyper-inflation as occurred in Germany in the 1920's, Hungary in the 1940's, Argentina in the 1980's, Yugoslavia in the 1990's, and Zimbabwe today." They don't pull their punches when they evaluate what is likely to occur.

The CBO report is most often cited as the definitive information source for financial analysis for early 2013. In fact, their report shows two likely scenarios for the United States economic conditions. In the primary scenario the government allows the changes scheduled under current law to occur. In the alternative scenario the government seeks to stimulate the economy by allowing some of the tax cuts to continue and also increase some sectors of the government spending.

In the primary scenario Congress does little or nothing to avoid the fiscal cliff. This causes financial tightening across most sectors of the United States economy leading to a probable recession starting in the summer of 2013. The CBO predicts a decline in the real GDP of approximately 0.5 percent and an increase in unemployment to about 9 percent. By 2022 this leaves us with a public debt of approximately 58% of the GDP.

The alternative scenario is a compromise, allowing some tax cuts or spending increases, while disallowing others. Under this alternative scenario the deficits are spread across a wider range of years, from 2013 out to 2022. The country would see a short-term growth in the economy of about 1.7 percent and an unemployment rate stabilizing near the current 8 percent level. However public debt would climb to ninety percent of the GDP by the fiscal year 2022, higher than any of us have ever seen in this country. More of our tax money would go to pay the interest on the national debt, which creates a less prosperous country. This is a spiraling national debt increase that cannot be sustained.

Very likely what really happens will be somewhere in the middle of these two scenarios (though that's certainly not guaranteed). No matter how we look at it, market volatility will increase, either in the near term or a few years further out. Bear in mind that in August, 2011, the market dropped by 7% and took six months to recover. We could see greater volatility than that. The market is probably not going to be a safe place to have your extra money. Unfortunately, it is the place where many of our pensions and IRA accounts are invested.

The credit rating of the United States has already been downgraded, and it might happen again. Though the direct impact of this does not affect the average American consumer, the ripples from such a downgrade would increase costs, especially for foreign goods.

No matter the scenario chosen or the decisions made by the government, there is little doubt that we will all face higher taxes and those tax increases will probably be permanent. Don't be fooled by political rhetoric. The wealthy in the United States could have all their possessions confiscated and applied to the national debt and the American people would still have a huge debt burden to shoulder.

We most certainly will see a small tax hike in January when Social Security will take out a bit more, back up to the previous 6.2% level.

Even if Congress defers that, they could come back later and retroactively renew it.

There will be reduced unemployment benefits. Jobs will become even harder to find and budgets will become tighter.

Here is the bottom line from the CBO. "Reductions in taxes or increases in spending in 2013, relative to what would occur under current law, would have near-term economic benefits but would add to the already large accumulation of government debt. Because current policies would ultimately lead to an unsustainable level of federal debt, policymakers will need – at some point – to adopt policies that will require people to pay significantly more in taxes, accept substantially less in government benefits and services, or both."

No matter how you slice this problem, what scenario you choose, or what decisions are made, Americans are going to be adversely impacted.

What is Congress doing? They are simply engaged in finger-pointing and name calling instead of taking action to benefit their constituents (that would be us). Personally we find it hard to believe that Republicans will not extend middle-income tax cuts for Americans and that the Democrats totally defeated a series of four Republican budget cuts in the summer of 2012.

Republicans complain that Democrats are over-taxing job creators and Democrats claim the Republicans are shielding the rich. While they bicker amongst themselves, the United States comes closer to the fiscal cliff.

What we can expect is that Congress will pass some stopgap measure to extend some of the tax benefits for several months. Don't let that make you complacent, though. There are many historical precedents for enacting tax laws that work retroactively.

The government will not be able to save you from much of the overspending accumulated over the last few decades. The future of our children and grandchildren is mortgaged. We will need to take on that burden ourselves. Fortunately, that's what Americans have always excelled at.

WHAT TO DO

You've just finished reading about a devastating financial crisis looming on the horizon. What can you do to prepare for it? What can you do to survive the aftermath?

The changes certainly look bleak, and the typical American family will face some trials in the near and long-term future, but don't panic. For most American families finances will be a little tighter but we can all learn to deal with that. You'll have to stay flexible, but there are some core principles you can adhere to right now (and they are good principles at any time).

No two people face exactly the same set of circumstances, so preparation is going to look different for each of us.

First of all, if you are employed keep your job if you can. That seems like common sense, but most of us have quit jobs before we have a new one lined up. In today's economy, that isn't a good plan. Before quitting your current job, have another job waiting for you.

Squirrel some money away. Skip the soda and put the money in a jar in your bedroom and it will quickly add up. It might not seem like a lot, but every little bit helps. If you are fortunate enough to have some extra money, we have more specific advice at the end of this section, but most of us still live from one paycheck to another. Make it a priority to put some of that money aside, though. As bad as this sounds, and as much as we hate to advise it, keep some cash in a safe place in your house. We don't usually advocate that; we like money to work for us (even at a paltry 0.75 percent APR). However, if the worst case scenario occurs (collapse of the national economy), banks will be put into forced holidays and you'll want money easily available. We're not saying that will happen, we simply suggest planning for the worst.

Not to sound extremist, but many conservative financial advisors (not to be confused with conservative politicians) point out that the FDIC is completely bankrupt, and over 400 banks[iv] went out of business over the last four years, even with the bailout monies. Keep some of your cash accessible outside your banking institution.

Most financial advisors say you should have a six month emergency fund set aside in case of a severe recession. We're not sure these advisors work in our neighborhood. We agree that six months of emergency cash would be ideal; it makes a good goal. You might have old gold or silver jewelry that you can sell. That sounds extreme, but the price for these precious metals is high right now, and it might be better to have cash tucked in the back of your dresser than Aunt Peggy's old silver necklace you never wear.

Pay down debt. This is a good idea at any time. When you are in debt, even to a credit card company, you are spending your hard earned money to support someone else. Some people say wait for the crash and don't worry about your debt, but you're the first person the bill collector will come to when the economy crashes. Get rid of debt. This isn't as complicated as it sounds. The internet abounds with methods to burn down your debt levels. If you have more than a single debt, choose the one with the highest interest and focus on eliminating it. Once that is paid off, apply the money from the first debt to the second one on your list, and so on. If you have credit card debt at high interest rates, try to find a lower interest credit card to roll the debt over or negotiate with your lender for a lower rate.

Avoid non-essential spending. After advising you to remove the debt in your life, this one should be perfectly obvious, but so many of us get stressed and go shopping. That won't help you. Get stressed and go for a walk or work in your garden (more on that in a moment). So skip the vacation and that new electronic gadget. Think Great Depression of the 1930's. We don't think it will be that bad, but it's still better to be prepared.

You must plan on an additional $2000 to $3500 in tax increases that the typical family faces in 2013. Working these numbers into your budget can only help. We hope that legislation mitigates the amount somewhat. If they do then you will have the opportunity to save more cash for the future.

Finding a way to reduce your fixed expenses will help extend your cash and ride out the recession, especially if you lose your job or take a cut in pay. Can you reduce the cost of your cell phone plan? Do you really need three hundred cable channels? Can you operate at a less expensive lower internet speed? Can you eliminate your land line?

Try the following to save some money:

Reduce your electric bill by turning off lights, correctly setting your thermostat, and unplugging devices that constantly draw current,

Reduce water usage by making sure your dishwasher is fully loaded, or wash only a few dishes by hand,

Water your yard less,

Set a time for taking showers (especially useful with teens in the house),

Turn down the temperature of your water heater,

Reduce clothing costs by shopping at resale shops,

Cut down on fast food (which also helps your health),

Pare grocery costs by comparing prices and using coupons, and

Limit trips to the grocery store to twice a week and use a shopping list, (which also helps eliminate impulse buying).

Start a garden. You don't need to plan on something that would rival the local farmers. If you don't have a large yard, or don't have much room for a garden just a two-foot square raised bed (two bags of dirt or a few shovels full) can provide you with tomatoes. Or you can use gardening pots to plant individual foods, especially if you have a small yard or simply an apartment patio. If you really want a lot of food from a small bed, raise some squash (from personal experience). A small garden makes you a little less dependent on the grocery store and fluctuating market prices, and it gets you back in touch with nature. Grandmother always said that the best therapy for hard times was getting your hands in the dirt and watching crops grow.

Make friends with your neighbors. Share this book with them (or have them buy it - thank you). If you're all talking about gardens it might make more sense to grow different foods. Our dear friend Jaki grows amazing tomatoes and we just haven't been able to manage a worthwhile batch of those. Did we mention squash? We can trade, and so can you. When our country faced tough times in the past, neighbors made all the difference. Some might be good at plumbing or carpentry or be able to help with your computer. Bartering opportunities abound if you're willing to look.

Review your retirement accounts, especially your plans at work. Contribute as much as you can to pre-tax investments. Taxes are supposed to go up and deductions go down, so contributing as much as possible to tax-deferred investments, like your IRA, 401(k) or a 529 education plan makes sense.

Talk to a good tax advisor and discuss converting your traditional IRA to a Roth IRA before the end of 2012, since you will pay taxes on what you convert. Calculate whether the costs of paying the lower taxes now are offset by the expected increased taxes when you retire. If you don't have the money to pay the taxes, don't do it.

Many analysts say it is time to diversify your income, especially if you work in the defense industry. Perhaps look for other sectors of the economy where you might be able to use what you know. Along those same lines, work on improving your skills. Some people we know took Continuing Education courses at the local community college to improve their computer skills. They are now more valuable to their employers, which is always a good thing.

American spirit has always been best exemplified by those willing to become entrepreneurs. A friend of ours now fixes boats and boat motors in his spare time. We started a business writing apps for mobile phones. There are many websites and excellent books on starting a small business[v] Now might be the time to do it, especially if you have a skill or hobby that you enjoy and that might make a good business.

If you are considering whether to rent or buy a home, that's a personal decision you must make. Rental has flexibility and avoids many home expenses. If you might lose your job, renting is good because you are flexible enough to move elsewhere for work. Buying a home has more expenses, but with such low interest rates, lock them in if you can.

Your doctor has said this for years, and now is the time to listen. Get healthy. Medical care will continue, but it will be costly. There are many hidden costs in the Affordable Care Act and some of them might affect you.

Of course, there are also many web sites which specialize in survival. They expect the utter collapse of civilization as we know it. That is certainly one extreme scenario, but not a probable one. Store some food, especially staples. Grow a garden, become as independent as you can. Keep some water available. You don't want it sitting around forever, but you should have some on hand. It wouldn't hurt to get a good water filter, found at most outdoor camping stores. Don't spend a lot though; remember, you're watching expenses.

Have on hand all the items you would normally store for any kind of catastrophe, like a hurricane, tornado or earthquake. Many web sites can provide lists of items you need. If the worst case happens, ask yourself what you would do for power. Do you have or need a backup generator or alternate energy system? Most likely not. In 2008 when our area was hit by Hurricane Ike our wonderful neighbors helped us until power was restored (thanks again, Luke!). This is simply another good reason to get to know your neighbors.

Survivalists go so far as recommending that you leave the city. That's a personal decision, of course. In 1999 when the Y2K scare was at its height many experts advised leaving the city and living in the country for the same reasons we would use now. If you recall New Year's Day of the year 2000 no catastrophes crashed on the heads of the American people. (Of course, there was a lot of corporate preparation for Y2K.) If society comes unraveled the city won't be a great place to be, but you can at least be prepared.

Survivalists also recommend self-defense training, and that is certainly not a bad idea. In times of trouble crimes rates almost always climb. Self-defense classes certainly cannot hurt.

As we said earlier, band with family, with neighbors and with friends to prepare for the fiscal cliff. Plant gardens together. Study self-help books and investment books together. If none of your family or friends will listen to you, then you must do a bit more preparation, because if our society implodes, you're the one they will come to. Even if the economy only slightly worsens, you'll be better prepared to handle adverse circumstances. You'll also be able to say you saw it coming.

WHAT TO DO IF YOU HAVE AN INVESTMENT PORTFOLIO

None of the following information is to be considered investment advice. Instead we've gathered broad-based concepts offered across a variety of investment advisors and tried to summarize this information. We're not making any guarantees and cannot be held liable for any investments anyone chooses to make. It is important to remember that no one cares about your money more than you do! Having covered that...

Buy and hold doesn't work as well any more. We've already seen portfolio values drop 30-40% twice since 1999. US Treasuries yields are at 1.4%, not even keeping up with inflation. These are not currently a wise investment.

Remember the maximum long-term capital gains tax will rise from 15% to 20%, which might not have significant impact on your personal income, but will very likely affect the market.

You may want to take some of your profits and losses in 2012 while the tax rates are lower and before the current tax cuts expire. This would mean selling stocks. On the positive side, this gives you cash if you need it. If you are able, this also provides money to invest if the market tumbles, which many forecasters predict will happen. It is never a good idea to manage a portfolio based solely on tax considerations, but it certainly makes sense to modify your investments to reduce tax burdens.

Diversifying your portfolio is always sound advice. Grandma always said don't keep all your eggs in one basket. Rebalance to handle your risk tolerance. The best idea might be simply exit the stock market, at least in the short term. Again, most analysts predict a rally after some period of time, although they cannot say with certainty how long it will take before the rally emerges. Bear in mind that the rally could be double digit, but you have to be in a position to buy to take advantage of stock increases.

Some people say to consider investing in municipal bonds. Others say that if the economy implodes that might not be a wise choice. Municipal bonds pay interest that is free of federal taxation.

Talk to your tax guy about all this and get some advice, tailored to your means, needs and goals.

At a bit over 2% inflation rate, cash is losing value. You need to be invested if you have the extra money. Some suggest investing in utilities, precious metals, mining stocks and related funds. With precious metals, you need to be able to handle the volatility.

If you want to stay invested, it wouldn't hurt to put your extra money into low volatility investments that are also dividend-paying stocks. Choosing the correct investments is the trick, though.

Finally, if you prepare well and the fiscal cliff isn't as bad as some predict it will be then you are still much better off and prepared for possible economic downturns.

WRAPPING IT UP

We did our research. We read hundreds of web sites and dozens of reports. We studied the scenarios built by the CBO and even went on to read (a few too many) survivalist web sites.

Like most of our family and many of our friends, we know that this great country is facing a fiscal dilemma. Extravagant government spending has to stop and the American people eventually have to be held accountable for the decades of government excess. Like most people, though, we thought maybe the problem would take care of itself over time.

We don't think so any more.

Even if Congress manages to sidestep the upcoming fiscal cliff in early 2013 this nation has a huge amount of accumulated debt that needs to be resolved. The interest that Americans pay on the debt is staggering. We can't even get a grasp of the amount. Already in just the first nine months of 2012 that interest expense is over $350 trillion dollars.[vi] There are 132 million households in the United States.[vii] Simple math says that just to pay the interest on the debt each family has to come up with over $2600. This amount doesn't even touch the principal on the interest. That just can't continue. This creates another, larger fiscal cliff looming on the further horizon.

WHO WE ARE

I'm Vince. I work in the defense industry, for a defense contractor. Yes, I'm a little worried about the "sequester" but there isn't a lot I can do about it except follow the same advice we give to you. I have a Master's degree in Studies of the Future. What's that, you ask? A Futurist is someone who studies the possible, probable and preferable futures along a rigidly defined field of study. In the case of this book, we studied the "fiscal cliff" and it scared us. I have a personal blog site, but I don't usually write about economic or political issues. Feel free to visit anyway: http://www.o-dark-thirty.blogspot.com/

I'm Marcella. I work with people in all areas of their lives. Some have financial troubles, others have emotional issues, some have physical problems. I have learned that we all have fears to face and it helps to have someone to share them with. When I first heard of the "fiscal cliff" I was curious. How can we prepare for this? That's what inspired this book. I love to pray for people; join me on Facebook if you like.

We wrote this book to help our family and our friends. We both sincerely hope this book helps you.

We encourage you to pray for our nation and may God bless you and your family.

END NOTES

i From the Tax Policy Center Data
http://www.taxpolicycenter.org/publications/url.cfm?ID=412666

ii From the Wikipedia page at
http://en.wikipedia.org/wiki/Gross_domestic_product

iii The Congressional Budget Office, or CBO, maintains all their reports at their website. It is available at http://www.cbo.gov/

iv FDIC maintains an up-to-date listing of failed banking institutions. It is available on-line at
http://www.fdic.gov/bank/individual/failed/banklist.html

v One site recommended The $100 Startup. Amazon has both the hard copy and the Kindle version. We haven't read it, but it does have over four stars on Amazon.

vi This is from the following government web site:
http://www.treasurydirect.gov/govt/reports/ir/ir_expense.htm

vii From the Quickfacts page of the Census Bureau found at
http://quickfacts.census.gov/qfd/states/00000.html

ABOUT THE AUTHORS

Vincent Bernhardt's other book, *My Mother-in-law Misadventures* is available on Amazon, Smashwords and other electronic publishing venues. It is a witty and occasionally poignant recollection of the decade spent living with his Mother-in-law under the same roof.
He likes writing on his blog at www.o-dark-thirty.blogspot.com.

Marcella Bernhardt is both an artist and author. She currently perfects her techniques and shares with family and friends.

www.ingramcontent.com/pod-product-compliance
Lightning Source LLC
Chambersburg PA
CBHW071603170526
45166CB00004B/1781